Witness to History

World War II Home Front

Gary E. Barr

Heinemann Library
Chicago, Illinois

Customer Service 888-454-2279
Visit our website at www.heinemannlibrary.com

Designed by Heinemann Library
Page layout by Ginkgo Creative, Inc.
Photo research by Bill Broyles
Printed and bound in China by South China
Printing Company Limited

08 07 06 05 04
10 9 8 7 6 5 4 3 2 1

**Library of Congress Cataloging-in-Publication
Data**
Barr, Gary, 1951-
   World War II home front / Gary Barr.
      p. cm. -- (Witness to history)
Summary: Provides an overview of what life was like in
the United States during World War II.
Includes bibliographical references (p.) and index.
   ISBN 1-4034-4571-0 -- ISBN 1-4034-4579-6 (pbk.)
   1. United States--History--1933-1945--Juvenile
literature. 2. United States--Social conditions--1933-
1945--Juvenile literature. 3. World War, 1939-1945--
United States--Juvenile literature. 4. World War, 1939-
1945--Social aspects--Juvenile literature. [1. World War,
1939-1945--United States. 2. United States--History--
1933-1945. 3. United States--Social conditions--1933-
1945. 4. World War, 1939-1945--Social aspects.] I. Title.
II. Series: Witness to history
(Heinemann Library (Firm))
   E806.B336 2004
   940.53'73--dc22
                                     2003018146

Acknowledgments
The author and publisher would like to thank the
following for permission to reproduce photographs:

pp. 5, 12, 14, 17, 35, 46 Bettmann/Corbis; pp. 7, 16, 22, 30
Library of Congress; pp. 9, 51 Franklin Delano Roosevelt
Library; p. 15 Courtesy of Carrie Radabaugh; pp. 19, 24,
25, 38, 40, 48 National Archives and Records
Administration; p. 21 AP Wide World Photos; p. 26
Walter Sanders/Time Life Pictures/Getty Images; pp. 28,
31, 42 Minnesota Historical Society; pp. 32, 45 Corbis;
pp. 34, 44 Frank Scherschel/Time Life Pictures/Getty
Images; p. 36 Lucien Aigner/Corbis

Cover photograph of female workers at Douglas
Aircraft's Long Beach, California, plant, reproduced
with permission of National Archives and Records
Administration.

The publisher would like to thank Guy LoFaro for his
help in the preparation of this book.

Every effort has been made to contact copyright
holders of any material reproduced in this book. Any
omissions will be rectified in subsequent printings if
notice is given to the publisher.

Some words are shown in bold,
like this. You can find out what
they mean by looking in the glossary.

Contents

Introduction

Huge battles, modern weapons, and military heroes usually dominate accounts of wars. Better weapons and supplies produced in the United States—far from the combat zones—did much to bring about victory in World War II. However, there are other factors in war. The United States home front during World War II had the biggest effect of any home front in world history so far.

Causes of World War II

World War II began in Europe in 1939. Though the United States did not enter the conflict until the Japanese attacked Pearl Harbor, Hawaii, on December 7, 1941. Japan, Germany, and Italy were on missions of conquest. The leaders of these three nations wanted to expand into other territories and acquire new sources of **raw materials** for their factories. Germany's Adolf Hitler, Italy's Benito Mussolini, and Japan's Hideki Tojo also believed their cultures were superior. By taking over other nations and replacing their way of life with their own, the leaders believed they would improve the lives of the conquered peoples.

Germany threatened war to force Czechoslovakia (present-day Czech Republic and Slovakia) and Austria to give up land. World War II started when Germany invaded Poland in 1939. Italy had already conquered the African country of Ethiopia, and Japan had previously seized part of China.

Up to this point, the United States had tried to stay out of the war. The U.S. followed a **policy** called **isolationism,** and refused to get involved in foreign wars. But President Franklin Delano Roosevelt and other leaders correctly predicted that the United States could not avoid the conflict. The leaders knew that U.S. trade and independence would eventually be disrupted. U.S. government leaders began preparing military forces long before the country entered the war. When Japan attacked Pearl Harbor on December 7, 1941, the location of the attack was a surprise. However, few government leaders were surprised that the United States had now been drawn into the war.

Factory production of war materials soared in the U.S. during World War II and contributed greatly to the country's success in the conflict.

The home front

As dramatic and unforgettable as World War II battle **campaigns** would become, the war was also fought by **civilians** on U.S. soil. People who stayed at home found ways to contribute to the fight against the Japanese and the **Nazis.** Factories employed thousands of workers to produce war supplies. Civilian leaders, families, and even children banded together to support the war effort in countless creative ways.

Some people believe that the only important aspect of a war is fighting and winning on the battlefield. But the actual words and experiences of those living on the home front during World War II make it clear that hard work, sacrifice, and optimism at home were equally important to the United States victory.

How Do We Know?

By studying history, we can learn about past events. For example, if we need to find out about the fall of the **Roman Empire** or the Norman invasion of England, we can find many books and articles about these subjects. Books and articles can tell us when and how the events took place and provide details about the important people. Books and articles often not only explain why things have happened—by examining the background of the events, but also how the events shaped the course of history.

Although books and articles can be helpful and informative, they are often written many years—sometimes hundreds of years—after the events they describe. And, like any story that is told secondhand, some changes, and even mistakes, can creep into the accounts. Perhaps a historian did not like Romans or military leaders. Such an attitude can affect how a historian tells a story because a historian may present the facts as he or she wanted them to occur. A historian might leave out facts that do not fit into his or her worldview. Such a personal opinion is called **bias,** and it makes some historical accounts unreliable.

On the other hand, a historian might have no personal opinion on the matter. However, he or she still relies on accounts that were written long after the events. Such accounts are called secondary sources because a historian arrives at them secondhand. Historians who base their writing on earlier retellings might repeat the bias or even the mistakes of the previous accounts. It is easy to see how this process can change a simple statement with each retelling.

Getting to the source

This book uses primary sources to tell the story of the United States home front during World War II. These are first-hand accounts of events. Historians dealing with events from long ago must rely on primary sources such as codes of law, church records, letters, journals, and diaries. Many people kept a record of the events from their point of view. Their first-hand accounts can give us an up-close, personal view of a time period in history.

Posters like this one can help us understand past ages. This poster encourages residents of Pennsylvania to volunteer for service on the home front.

The purpose of history

Studying history helps us learn how people dealt with various problems. Such an understanding can allow us to deal with related problems that we face today—and will face in the future. So many people recorded their thoughts during World War II that we can benefit from exposure to opinions from a number of different perspectives.

Franklin D. Roosevelt: Before 1941

Franklin Delano Roosevelt was president of the United States during World War II. He was born to a wealthy New York family in 1882. He graduated from law school and practiced law in New York before being elected senator in 1910.

Disease and political success

In 1921, at the age of 39, Roosevelt fell seriously ill with a disease called **polio.** He survived, but never walked again without the assistance of leg braces and canes. However Roosevelt found a way to live with his handicap. He exercised the parts of his body that were not crippled. He also had machines specially designed to assist him— even a car that operated by using hand controls. He wore leg braces so that he could stand when he made speeches. In 1932, Roosevelt was elected president of the United States. Many felt that his struggle with polio gave him the mental toughness he would later need to lead the country through the **Great Depression** and a world war.

Promoting peace and supporting allies

At the outbreak of World War II in Europe in 1939, Americans were opposed to getting involved. Countless U.S. soldiers had been killed in World War I (1914–1918) and Americans believed that conflict had done little to promote lasting peace. Roosevelt supported public opinion. But when Great Britain became desperate for supplies in the early years of World War II, he found a way to send them goods and allow them to pay later. This was called the **Lend-Lease Act.** Meanwhile, Roosevelt continually warned Japan to stop its attacks on nations in east Asia. But on December 7, 1941, the Japanese launched a surprise attack against the United States in Pearl Harbor, Oahu, Hawaii. On December 8, the United States declared war on Japan.

Roosevelt's State of the Union address

Roosevelt addressed the U.S. Congress and the American people in his **State of the Union address** on January 6, 1942. He outlined the amount of weapons and supplies that the United States would need to produce for the war effort.

As we sit here at home contemplating our own duties let us think and think hard of the example which is being set for us by our fighting men. . . . We must raise our sights all along the production line. Let no man say it cannot be done. . . . the production people can do it, if they really try. . . . These figures [of weapons and supplies] will give the Japanese and the **Nazis** a little idea of just what they accomplished at Pearl Harbor. . . . The militarists of Berlin and Tokyo started the war, but the massed, angered forces of common humanity will finish it.

Franklin D. Roosevelt was president longer than any other person—he served twelve and a half years.

Franklin D. Roosevelt: 1941-1945

The last four years of Franklin D. Roosevelt's life were spent leading the United States through World War II. The United States declared war on Japan following their attack on Pearl Harbor. This led to Germany and Italy—the other **Axis Powers** along with Japan—declaring war on the United States. Suddenly, President Roosevelt was **commander in chief** of the country's military in a global conflict.

Leadership on the home front

During World War II, Roosevelt left much of the war strategy to capable leaders such as General George C. Marshall, supreme commander of the U.S. military; General Dwight D. Eisenhower, the top U.S. general in Europe; and General Douglas MacArthur, the top military leader in the war against Japan. Meanwhile, President Roosevelt worked to maintain good relations between its main **allies,** including Great Britain and the Soviet Union. He also worked toward keeping Americans on the home front united, well-informed, and committed to producing goods needed for the war effort.

Roosevelt's qualities

Roosevelt was an inspirational leader. During the darkest days of the **Great Depression** he told people, "[t]he only thing we have to fear is fear itself." Now during the desperate world-wide struggle of World War II, he motivated both soldiers and workers. Roosevelt spoke in a clear, confident voice when he addressed Americans. He compared World War II to the early years of the **Revolutionary War,** when George Washington and the Continental Army were faced with formidable odds. He pointed to Washington's ability to persevere despite great hardships, resulting in victory and the creation of the United States. As World War II progressed, Roosevelt urged Americans onward, telling them it was only a matter of time until the fighting spirit of the **Allied Powers,** combined with America's ability to produce goods, would overwhelm the Axis Powers.

A Fireside Chat

Roosevelt began making regular speeches to the nation on the radio in 1933. These talks came to be known as Fireside Chats. Nearly 80 percent of American adults heard Roosevelt's Fireside Chat on the radio on the evening of February 23, 1942. In the speech, Roosevelt explained why America's most important job at that moment was to produce as many weapons and supplies as possible.

Our first job then is to build up production—uninterrupted production—so that the United Nations can maintain control of the seas and attain control of the air—not merely a slight superiority, but an overwhelming superiority.... We are calling for new plants and ... additions to old plants. We are calling for plant conversion to war needs. We are seeking more men and more women to run them. We are working longer hours. We are coming to realize that one extra plane or extra tank or extra gun or extra ship completed tomorrow may, in a few months, turn the tide on some distant battlefield; it may make the difference between life and death for some of our own fighting men. We know now that if we lose this war it will be generations or even centuries before our conception [idea] of democracy can live again. And we can lose this war only if we slow up our effort....

Conducting the War

Franklin D. Roosevelt did much to motivate Americans to work hard. At the same time, countless other government leaders were responsible for turning the United States into a productive home front. For example, members of U.S. Congress agreed with President Roosevelt that emergency measures had to be taken.

Car factories were ordered by the government to begin producing military machines, and laws made **strikes** by workers illegal. To raise money, the tax system was changed and the rich were taxed at a higher-than-normal rate. Several **government agencies** were created to make sure the new system worked efficiently.

Government officials at the national, state, and local levels contributed to the war effort. One of the main ways in which all three levels were involved concerned **"civil defense."** Civil Defense was largely responsible for guarding borders and preparing U.S. citizens for possible enemy attacks.

Citizens were trained by government officials to identify potential acts of **sabotage.** People were required to participate in bomb drills in case of attack. They were also shown how to hang **blackout curtains** to prevent enemy bombers from seeing lighted buildings at night. Fortunately, most of this training was not needed. But the country was prepared nonetheless.

During World War II, Americans believed enemy bombers might attack the country. Here, two women hang blackout curtains.

Thomas Scott's mission
Thomas Scott worked as a Civil Defense Volunteer in the Philadelphia, Pennsylvania, area.

Our mission was to protect the Home Front. . . . One of our responsibilities as an air raid warden was to make sure everybody had their lights turned out at night and that people weren't wandering around without any place to go. Bombing attacks in Europe occurred at night because it was hard for weapons of the time to shoot down attack planes, and people "wandering around" might be spies.

Another of our duties was to have one or two wardens on alert at all times to watch for anything that might happen in the neighborhood—like suspicious strangers wandering around [watching for spies or terrorists].

Sheril Jankovsky Cunning's memories
Sheril Jankovsky Cunning was a child growing up in Long Beach, California, during the war.

I lived constantly with the fear we might be invaded or bombed. . . . My father was the block air raid warden. I'll never forget the fear I felt as he went out during air raid alerts and left the family huddled in the hallway. The sirens would go off, the searchlights would sweep the sky, and Daddy would . . . go out to protect the neighborhood.

Recruiting Efforts

World War II was a huge conflict. Roosevelt knew that millions of U.S. citizens would be needed to fight and prepare for the war. In the end, about sixteen million volunteers, draftees, and military professionals served in uniform at one time or another during World War II.

Thousands of women and men volunteered to serve in World War II. Encouraged by radio and newspaper ads, they felt it was their duty to defend their country. But many people had families and career obligations that made it difficult for them to leave. To force larger numbers of people into service, Congress enacted a draft.

Under the draft system, all men in the United States between the ages of 21 and 35 were required to register with the federal government. Each was then given a physical to ensure he was healthy enough to fight, and was assigned a random number. Next, a lottery drawing was held. If a man's number was picked as one of the first in the lottery, he would most likely have to go fight. Later in the war, all men aged eighteen and over were required to register with the government, and the lottery system was abandoned. The government simply started sending men to fight based on their age. The older the man, the less likely it was he would be sent to fight.

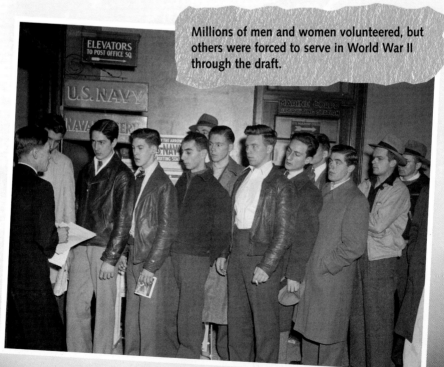

Millions of men and women volunteered, but others were forced to serve in World War II through the draft.

W. Lloyd Warner's account
On the day recruits left small towns for basic training, there were huge sendoffs. W. Lloyd Warner described such a sendoff from Jonesville, Illinois.

At 6:30 [A.M.] a crowd of people gathered outside a local café where the selectees [recruits] were having their breakfast and receiving final instructions. Outside, the high school band would fall into position and next a color guard from the American Legion. As the boys came out of the door of the café, they lined up and the head of the draft board called "forward march." They marched down Liberty Street to the railroad station where a large crowd had gathered.

Everywhere little groups of people surrounded individuals about to leave. As the train would come around the curve from the west the conversation picked up in intensity and the band begin to play. Hurried kisses, embraces, and handshakes from relatives and friends. One by one the boys shook hands with the draft board and climbed onto the train. The train pulled out and the buzz of excitement in the crowd was drowned out by the band playing the Marine Hymn. Within a minute or two the station became deserted except for the two men loading mail and baggage onto a truck. Jonesville had made another contribution to the war.

War often meant that children had to be separated from their fathers, and sometimes their mothers. Here, U.S. soldier Dorr Radabaugh poses with his son, Dennis, at Fort Still in Oklahoma in September 1944.

Financing the War

Fighting a war at several distant locations at the same time cost billions of dollars. Soldiers had to have clothes, food, and weapons. Ships, planes, trucks, tents, medical supplies, and countless other supplies and equipment were also required. How did the United States pay for all of this?

War bonds were an important means of **financing** the war. The bonds allowed the government to receive loans from Americans who bought the bonds. Later, the government would pay back the money with **interest.** By the end of the war, citizens had purchased more than $135 billion worth of war bonds.

Taxes are always a main source of income for governments. **Income tax** is a payment to a government based on individuals' wages. Governments that use this type of tax normally have two beliefs. First, they believe that people who earn higher wages should be taxed at a higher rate because it will not cause them hardship. Second, they believe that wealth from income should be leveled to prevent people from becoming extremely poor or extremely rich. During World War II, the U.S. government taxed the rich at even higher rates than normal. Most did not complain, believing that it was a major way they could help the war effort.

Posters and other ads encouraged Americans to buy war bonds—and people did, in huge amounts.

Taxes and war bonds were two of the most important sources of money for the war. Still, the U.S. government simply could not pay all of its expenses. By the end of the war, the government was in debt to thousands of companies.

BUY WAR BONDS

Shirley Hackett's reflections

Shirley Hackett had been working at a telephone company. But when the war began, she took a job at a factory that made ball bearings. Here, she talks about the transformation the country underwent in the early years of the war.

In less than a year I watched the United States transformed from a peaceful country to an enormous manufacturing nation, from having Sunday picnics together to buckling down several days a week to build what was needed for the war. You don't know what this country can do when people are pulling together, breaking their necks to do what they can.

There was a great coming together of people, working as a team, being proud of what you were doing because you knew it was contributing something to the war effort. Everybody did their share, from the oldest gentleman on the street who was working as an air raid warden and watching over us during blackouts to little children who saved things that were crucial at that time—paper, tin cans, scrap, anything that could be reused for the war. Buying war bonds was almost like breathing. I don't recall many people who didn't have them.

A girl scout who posed for a war poster had the honor of meeting Eleanor Roosevelt.

We all pulled together in a way that I have never seen happen any other time in this country.

Advertising the War

The United States government strongly urged people to work hard on the war effort. In many cases leaders praised the work of Americans, while strongly criticizing its war enemies. The government advertised the war as a way to gain support for it.

For the most part, advertising the war emphasized its positive aspects. Typical **slogans** used were "Man the Guns, Bring Home our Boys," and a figure known as Uncle Sam stating, "I Want You for the U.S. Army." Posters featured images of handsome, heroic soldiers and beautiful, hardworking women.

Sometimes negative **racist** images were used to encourage hatred of America's enemies. Some were mild, such as posters with an image of Hitler or other **Axis Power** leaders with the caption, "This Is the Enemy." Other images were more extreme, and referred to enemies in racist terms: Germans were called *Huns* and Japanese were called *Japs*. Unfortunately, using such methods created hatred in the U.S. of many loyal, patriotic German Americans and Japanese Americans.

The government also used **propaganda,** a type of information that usually exaggerates or even misrepresents facts to influence public opinion. Huge posters depicted grand battle scenes, used catchy slogans, and showed images of Uncle Sam asking if you were doing your part to support troops. Other pictures depicted Germans, Japanese, and Italians as evil villains ready to kill innocent women and children.

How effectively did these war advertisements influence U.S. citizens? Some of the positive messages probably inspired Americans to enlist in the armed forces or to work harder at their jobs. However, many people believe the negative, racist ads caused much hatred and fear among citizens.

United We Win

This poster is an example of the positive advertising the U.S. government published in support of the war. Two men of different races come together in order to produce supplies for the **Allied Powers.**

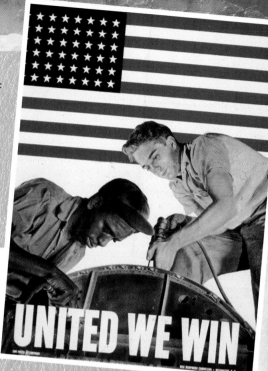

Warning!

This poster includes negative **stereotypes** the U.S. government used in an attempt to make citizens fear Japan and Germany and rally against them. The stereotyping worked: many Japanese Americans and German Americans were feared, mistrusted, and **discriminated** against during the war.

Eleanor Roosevelt

Eleanor Roosevelt, the wife of President Franklin D. Roosevelt and the niece of President Theodore Roosevelt, was a shy girl from New York who became one of America's most famous women. Eleanor contributed to many charitable causes, wrote a newspaper column, promoted women's rights, took a leading role in the promotion of racial equality, and spoke to a number of groups rallying support for the war and other programs. After her husband's death in 1945, she became the U.S. **ambassador** to the **United Nations.** Few other first ladies could match these accomplishments.

A shy girl

Eleanor was from one of the United States's most prominent families, but she was not highly pursued by young men. Her shyness and lack of great beauty hid a warm, caring, and intelligent person. During family visits, Eleanor and her distant relative Franklin gradually became friends. After dating several beautiful and popular girls, Franklin finally recognized the beauty within Eleanor. When Eleanor was nineteen they became engaged and the couple was married two years later.

A national figure

Eleanor was a supportive companion during Franklin's hectic political career and his fight against **polio.** She soon became interested in several charitable and other organizations. She helped form the National Youth Organization, which assisted poor children during the **Great Depression;** worked with the National Association for the Advancement of Colored People (NAACP); and was active in several women's groups, including the Women's League of Voters and the Women's Trade Union League. In one 12-year period she helped write 2,500 newspaper columns, wrote 299 magazine articles, published 6 books, and made more than 840 speeches.

Like any public figure, however, Eleanor had critics. Many men, and even some women, thought that a president's wife should stay in the background and that it was not ladylike for her to be a public leader. Eleanor considered her work to be too important to care about such criticisms. In many ways she was one of the first modern women of the United States.

Eleanor Roosevelt on fear

Eleanor Roosevelt was fearless when it came to opinions of her work. Her nontraditional role as a wife gave strength to other women looking to contribute to the war effort.

You gain strength, courage and confidence by every experience in which you really stop to look fear in the face. You are able to say to yourself, "I have lived through this horror. I can take the next thing that comes along." You must do the thing you think you cannot do.

Eleanor Roosevelt on service

Eleanor came from a family that placed much value on volunteer work and community service.

I could not at any age be content to take my place in a corner by the fireside and simply look on.

Eleanor Roosevelt worked tirelessly for many worthy causes in the 1930s and 1940s. She may have been our greatest first lady.

Factory Production

Millions of women and men were in the military during World War II, greatly reducing the labor force in the United States. People moved from farms to work in factories. White males of western European ancestry had dominated U.S. businesses for years. African Americans, women, and other **minorities** had previously been denied opportunities, but were now welcomed in American factories.

Wartime conversion

Not enough factories produced war supplies at the beginning of the war. Part of the solution to this problem was for existing plants to convert—that is, to change what they were currently making. For example, typewriter companies began producing bullets, auto-makers began building tanks, and clothing factories sewed military uniforms.

War production increases

U.S. workers on the home front met the challenge—factory output nearly doubled and farm production rose by almost 25 percent during the war years. In 1944 alone, U.S. factories produced almost 100,000 aircraft and similar numbers of trucks, jeeps, and tanks. Efficiency increased so much that the time needed to build a large ship dropped from one year to less than two months.

Late in the war, the United States matched the combined production of Japan, Germany, and Italy.

Don Johnson's account
Don Johnson was a factory worker during World War II.

It was a time of your life when you saw there really wasn't any way that you could do anything else but hang on to the goal that you had a part to play, and you would persevere and do that part. It was a period when American industry had the greatest increase in productivity of all time. I believe, in large measure, it was because we as a nation were threatened. We were in a survival mode. People knew that, and they worked together to get the job done. We had a common purpose. We worked as a team. We had the skills. We had the machinery. We had the materials. We had the know-how. We achieved. And I believe given a similar set of circumstances, we could do it again.

A rule was established that said, "You can do it if you put forth the effort." I learned that rule during the war and it never left me … Expectations of their [people's] performances were raised, and people responded. Many of those people still carry those skills, those drives, with them. A frequent phrase used by Americans was, "We are all in this together."

Rosie the Riveter

Women filled jobs traditionally held by men during World War II. They worked on production lines, in steel mills, on the docks, and at jobs that required heavy manual labor. Women also took over other male-dominated positions, such as bus and truck drivers, train conductors, lumberjacks, and barbers.

To encourage females to take on traditionally male jobs, the United States government created a **symbolic** character named Rosie the Riveter. Posters usually portrayed Rosie as an attractive young woman heroically working in a factory.

New opportunities

By the time World War II broke out, machines were used at virtually every important job. Physical strength was not as important in the workplace, yet women were still denied access to many occupations. When masses of men left to fight, factories were desperate for workers. Many male managers had little faith in women's abilities, but they decided to try employing them. Quick courses of training were used to prepare women for jobs operating machinery. Then male managers watched closely to see if females could do their jobs properly. Women responded magnificently. Ignoring rude comments and lower pay, they proved their abilities in a variety of industrial positions. By the end of the war any woman acting as "Rosie" was a hero.

Rosie the Riveter helped women realize that they could do something more with their lives.

Frankie Cooper's experience

Frankie Cooper worked as a crane operator in a steel mill during World War II.

The hardest part for me was sanding the rails. The rails are what the wheels of the crane run on. They're way up in the air over the concrete floor, and they have to be sanded every eight-hour shift . . . when I found out that the operators had to sand them I was almost scared to death. I thought, I can't do that. I can't look down at that concrete and put this little bucket of sand up and down . . . And one of the men said, "Well, that'll get her. She'll never sand them tracks." That's what made me sand them. After that I had to. I had to show them I could do it. . . . Every time a war comes along women take up non-traditional work again . . . World War II it was exactly the same thing, but the women were different in World War II: they didn't want to go back home and many of them didn't. And if they did go back home, they never forgot, and they told their daughters, "You don't have to be just a homemaker. You can be anything you want to be."

In this photo, women work on a B-17F bomber, also known as the "Flying Fortress," at an aircraft company in Long Beach, California.

Women on the Home Front

Women played a vital role on the home front during World War II. Thousands of housewives replaced men on the job when their husbands left to fight. Numerous women felt they were just as good as men at these jobs, and they liked their new occupations. When men returned and reclaimed their positions from females, women had to go back to being housewives. However, they began striving for increased acceptance of females in the workplace and in United States society.

Traditional roles

For thousands of years women had been denied equal status to men. Much of this came from the fact that most females were not as physically strong as most men. Traditional occupations such as farming depended on physical strength and because of this, men were felt to be more important. While men have been stronger and brought home more money, women normally worked longer hours. By the 1940s, females often had part-time jobs while taking care of children and completing numerous household chores.

Resentment by males

With so many men fighting in World War II, there simply were not enough workers for the wide range of jobs available. Even though women performed well in the workplace during the war, the world was still dominated by males. But women did not forget their accomplishments during World War II. Almost all encouraged their daughters to strive for equality. The daughters listened. They would lead the fight for equal treatment in the United States between women and men in the workplace, in government, and in countless other ways in the 1950s and 1960s.

People often provided food for the war effort from their **victory gardens** without being paid.

Sybil Lewis's reflections

Sybil Lewis, an African-American woman living in Los Angeles, California, responded to an ad in the newspaper that offered to train women to do defense work during the war.

I grew up in Sapulpa, Oklahoma, a small town about fifteen miles [24 kilometers] from Tulsa . . . It was a very poor town and very **segregated.** All the blacks lived on the north side of town, across the railroad tracks, and the whites lived in the south part of town. Our parents made it very clear that we stayed on our side of the railroad tracks. You only crossed them if you had some business to go to in town, then you came right back.

Sybil heard that things were better in California. When her sister moved to Los Angeles, Sybil soon followed, hoping to get a good job.

[T]hey put me to work in the plant riveting small airplane parts, mainly gasoline tanks. The war years had a tremendous impact on women. I know for myself it was the first time I had a chance to get out of the kitchen and work in industry and make a few bucks. This was something I had never dreamed would happen. In Sapulpa [Oklahoma] all that women had to look forward to was keeping house and raising families . . . This was the beginning of women's feelings that they could do something more.

Farm Production

Farmers suffered greatly in the **Great Depression** of the 1930s.
Several had to sell their farms and move to cities. In the Midwest,
a serious drought complicated matters and created **dust bowl**
conditions. When World War II began, life for farm families changed
drastically. For the first time in more than ten years farmers began
seeing significant profits. They could now afford many goods formerly
too expensive a few years before.

Food for allies

Germany had cut many trade routes to Great Britain and other
countries. One of the few nations that could get food and supplies to
these nations was the United States. Supplies were especially vital to
the British because their cool climate and limited farmland made them
unable to produce all the food they needed.

To produce even more food in the U.S., people grew **victory gardens**.
People helped supply food by planting on land where gardening was
not normally done. Backyards, land near highways, and even front
lawns of courthouses were planted with crops.

Supplying millions of soldiers and personnel overseas required huge
amounts of agricultural goods. Foods normally come to mind as
agricultural goods, but there are many others. Materials such as
cotton and wool were used for clothing, tents, and even parachutes.

World War II
meant record
profits for farmers.
Feeding millions
of soldiers
allowed some
farmers to triple
their income.

When we moved back to the farm from California, it soon became apparent that the status of the farmer had changed. Where before we had been looked down upon, now we were important and looked up to because we were a crucial industry. We had to feed our country.

Manpower became crucial. Anybody who could carry a hoe or drive a team or a tractor helped out. They let schools out in the fall to help with the harvest and other times when necessary, and the teachers helped, too. Families helped each other. I worked all the time other than going to school. I pitched hay, hauled beans, picked spuds [potatoes]. When I was fifteen years old I picked four hundred half-sacks of spuds a day. And I mean that is a man's work, but you had the incentive to do it. It was patriotic and you got well paid besides.

As farm prices got better and better, the farmers suddenly became the wealth of the community.... We also started buying more things from the store ... A few of the women even started going into beauty parlors and getting their hair done.

Rationing

Because the United States military required huge quantities of supplies, people had to use less or even do without many items. This was partially because factories could not supply goods both to the **civilians** and the military. The government set up a system to restrict people's use of some goods. This system was called **rationing**.

Under rationing, the government issued people a stamp or other identification source. When the owner of a store saw this, he or she would allow a person to buy a limited amount of certain goods. Meat, butter, sugar, and gasoline were some of the important goods rationed. The government also set limits on the tin cans, waste paper, and aluminum that people could buy. In some cases, a person could only buy essential items—such as gasoline—on certain days. People sometimes complained, but they usually accepted the system because they knew it was helping the war effort.

People also practiced recycling. When articles of clothing tore or fell apart, people found ways to sew pieces together and make another useful object. Great amounts of rubber for vehicle tires were also reused. Children got involved going door-to-door to ask neighbors and townspeople to donate such goods. Once, in response to a request by President Roosevelt, Boy Scouts across the country gathered more than 54,000 tons (49,000 metric tons) of rubber for recycling.

Children were proud to help in the war effort. Here children donate scrap metal that can be reprocessed into useful products.

Vernon Sietmann's memories
Vernon Sietmann lived in Marshall County, Iowa, during the war years.

They [Americans] also put up with the few deprivations [things they lacked] the war put upon them: ration stamps and shortages of butter, gasoline, textiles [cloth], meat, cigarettes, automobiles and automobile tires, apartments, refrigerators—the list went on and on . . . all too often shoppers were wearily reminded: "Don't ya know there's a war on!"

There was a great shortage of supplies during the war where I lived in Marshall County, Iowa. Automobile and truck tires, farm equipment, and many more items were under federal regulation . . . Tires were rationed and very hard to get . . .

There were scrap drives organized in the county, and on a certain day people would get together and make an effort to bring in all the surplus [extra supplies] they could find. In our courthouse square in Marshalltown we had four or five old Civil War cannons, and even they were sent in and melted down for the war effort. That was quite a sacrifice, but that was how strong the feeling of cooperation was for the war effort.

Young people collect newspapers that will be recycled.

In the Cities

During the 1930s, U.S. cities had struggled through the **Great Depression.** Many factories shut down, putting people out of work. When World War II began in December 1941, there were suddenly jobs for everyone. The government paid companies to produce the huge amounts of weapons and supplies needed to fight the war.

People flocked to the cities for jobs. Teenagers from farms, wives of men serving in the war, members of **minority** groups, and the formerly unemployed were all part of this migration. Working side-by-side, these groups helped production soar. In many cases members of these various groups formed friendships, but in other cases **prejudice** against women and minorities remained.

Cities became lively places. Besides the industrial activity, theaters and other entertainment facilities were very active. Front porches and stoops became popular gathering places. From these sites neighbors enjoyed exchanging local gossip during free time while children played nearby.

Minority groups gained respect for their abilities by working side-by-side with whites during World War II.

Frankie Cooper's memories
Frankie Cooper recalls her part in the great migration to the cities. She was from Richmond, Kentucky.

In the spring of 1942, after the war had been going a little while, we decided to move

In order for my husband and I both to have jobs we had to go to an industrial section of the nation, so we moved to East St. Louis, Illinois.

I was twenty-one years old and had never worked before. My first job was at the American Steel foundry, in Granite City, Illinois, right outside St. Louis . . .

It was a great change from Richmond [Kentucky]. I had electricity and indoor plumbing. I just walked across the street to the grocery store. I had money to buy any kind of food I wanted. We had a secondhand car, so we didn't have to walk anymore. We went to the movies occasionally. We even went out to eat, which was brand-new to me. I had never done that.

Sybil Lewis remembers
Sybil Lewis, an African American, had been working as a welder. Even though she did an excellent job, she was replaced by a white woman.

I worked for a while as a riveter with this white girl, when the boss came around one day and said, "We've decided to make some changes." At this point he assigned her to do the riveting and me to do the bucking [using a bar to smooth out rivets]. I wanted to know why. He said, "Well, we just interchange once in a while." But I was never given the riveting job back. That was the first encounter I had with **segregation** in California, and it didn't sit too well with me . . . I wasn't failing as a riveter–in fact, the other girl learned to rivet from me–but I felt they gave me the job of bucker because I was black.

33

The Family

Though many sacrifices were necessary, Americans did not suffer from bombing raids (attacks by airplanes dropping explosives), hunger, and fear as the British, French, and many other countries did during World War II.

Record numbers of American teenagers married hastily, often right before a young man went off to war. Children of the 1930s and 1940s gained a special appreciation for the efforts of their parents. Years later many would look back on the sacrifices their mothers and fathers made during both the **Great Depression** and World War II. When they started families of their own, they were inspired by their parents actions. A typical attitude became "I want my children to have more than I had when I was a child."

Families were eager for good news of relatives. Saying a blessing or speaking of loved ones at an evening meal took on special meaning, while some members were far away engaged in the war.

Many couples who were already engaged married earlier if war was to separate them.

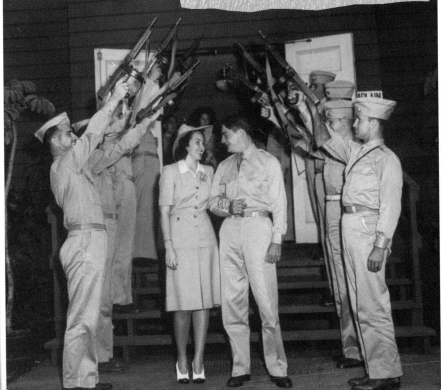

The Wood family remembers

Four of five sons in Albert and Louise Wood's family fought during World War II. One day, the family received a telegram that they knew bore bad news.

REGRET TO INFORM YOU YOUR SON STAFF SERGEANT FRANCIS F WOOD SERIOUSLY WOUNDED IN ACTION . . .

Fears of what was happening to the boys haunted the Wood family. Staying busy was their best therapy. Mrs. Wood even printed a family newsletter.

The boys all survived. Francis had a huge scar from a chest wound he received, but the others had not been wounded. For a while they went their separate ways, but eventually the sons reunited and worked in the father's business. He renamed it "Albert Wood & Five Sons."

Letters from loved ones serving overseas were almost always welcomed by family members and friends.

Children

Being a child during World War II was a unique experience and left a lasting impression. Many children grew up knowing their fathers only by photos taken before they marched off to war. Their childhood was an anxious time for fear of what might happen, and the harsh reality that family members were sometimes killed in the war. Though parents tried, there was no real escape from news of the war and its horrors. Play and other activities allowed children to forget about the war at times.

Children assisted in the war effort. Many gathered household items to donate for military use and contributed their nickels to pay for **war bonds.** Sometimes these efforts were school projects or activities encouraged by parents, in other cases children participated on their own.

Countless children made major contributions through writing. They wrote letters to women and men fighting in the war. Both the soldiers who received the letters and the young children who wrote them felt the letters were very important in their lives. Some soldiers kept every one of these letters.

Russia was an important U.S. **ally** during World War II. Here a girl makes a poster supporting Russia.

Jean Barr's memories

Jean Barr was in the seventh grade when the United States entered World War II.

Pearl Harbor ... war. It sounded exciting. I felt afraid. What does it all mean? These were my initial reactions as I walked home from school. The date was December 7, 1941, and I was twelve years old.

Soon I understood some of the reality; some my parents explained. Some of my uncles were leaving for military training. Civilians in our town volunteered. They helped conduct defense alert drills.

I was accustomed to seeing my mother in bright, freshly laundered house dresses. Now she wore overalls to work full-time in defense work at a cement plant nearby.

Our Girl Scout troop collected tons of newspapers for recycling. Each of us was assigned a serviceman. We wrote to him expressing our appreciation for his military service. Also we included current events taking place in our hometowns. The servicemen seemed to enjoy the letters and answered them when possible.

I vividly recall my Uncle Ed's homecoming. The whole family gathered on the large front porch, anticipating his arrival. Ed appeared walking, then running up the porch steps. He and his father embraced for several minutes. We all took a turn for a hug. Tears of joy and relief were all around us. I was now seventeen.

African Americans

In the 1940s most African Americans were treated like second-class citizens. They had to go to separate schools, work at lower paying jobs, and use separate public facilities. **Segregation** and **discrimination** were very strong, especially in the southern states. Would the war improve their situation?

When World War II began, thousands of African Americans volunteered to fight. Black leaders were quick to point out that these men were risking their lives for American freedom—freedom that was limited for blacks in their own country. They not only fought, but also produced heroes. Dorie Miller received the Medal of Honor for his actions at Pearl Harbor. Under heavy fire from Japanese planes, Miller—a cook who was not trained for combat—bravely fired back with an **anti-aircraft gun.** The Tuskegee Airmen, an African-American air force unit, fought with extreme bravery and great efficiency during World War II. Countless other blacks fought with great passion as well.

Meanwhile at home, African Americans were proving their capabilities and desires to excel in the workplace. Now working side-by-side in factories, whites saw that African Americans had the ability to do anything whites did. Blacks worked hard to take advantage of these new opportunities.

The superior performance of African Americans both on the battlefield and on the job resulted in more respect. Inspired by such performances, blacks began pressing for equal treatment in U.S. society. Unfortunately, **prejudice** and discrimination did not cease among most of America's white population. Throughout the south and in much of the north, blacks could not vote and segregation continued. It would take years of strong protests and court battles for African Americans to make serious gains.

American society had become so segregated that whites had little confidence in blacks' employment opportunities.

Alexander Allen's account
Alexander Allen was an African American living in Baltimore, Maryland, during the war.

When the war began, there were a number of blacks who were not enthusiastic about fighting it. They were sensitive to the inconsistency of a country that professed to be fighting for democracy and yet was not practicing it at home. But I felt then, and still feel, that the future of American blacks in this country, and that our destiny is bound up with the destiny of the rest of the United States.

I was in Cleveland [Ohio] in school with [African-American Olympic gold-medal winner] Jesse Owens, and I remember when Hitler left the stadium at the 1936 Olympics because Jesse had defeated the best that Aryan society [a superior, white, European race according to Hitler] had been able to produce. So blacks were aware of what was wrong with Hitler and what was wrong with [Italian dictator] Mussolini and understood the reason for opposing the **Nazi** war machine as it began to take one country after another in Europe. But at the same time, blacks were extremely concerned over the fact that racism and **bigotry** and discrimination were a continuing practice in this country. **Fascism** was not a monopoly of Hitler, or of Mussolini, or the Japanese. It was something that we saw every day on the streets of Baltimore and in other places. We did not see much sense in the war unless it was tied to a commitment for change on the domestic scene. It made a mockery of wartime goals to fight overseas . . . only to come back to the same kind of discrimination and racism here in this country.

The Media

World War II was well-named. Fighting took place all over the world. War raged in European cities, across Russian plains, in Asian jungles, on islands of the Pacific Ocean, across deserts of North Africa, and in **death camps** where millions of Jews were murdered. With control of the world at stake and loved ones fighting, the people of the United States wanted to hear what was happening. The media did their best to provide coverage of the wide-ranging events.

Reporters close to the fighting sent back daily accounts for use by the media. Popular reporters became some of the most famous people of the time. People trusted war correspondents, or reporters, such as Edward R. Murrow, Ernie Pyle, and others to tell them what was happening in the conflict. Newspapers, which were inexpensive and provided good detail, were also very popular. On special occasions British Prime Minister Winston Churchill or President Roosevelt would be on the radio. Just about every week Roosevelt made a short radio speech he called a Fireside Chat.

Movies were also well liked and affordable during the war years. Filmmakers near the combat zone sent back moving pictures that could be shown in theaters. These **newsreels,** accompanied by narrated descriptions, would be shown before the featured movie. Newsreels often offered the best images people could see of World War II. They were like mini news reports about the war and major world events.

Television was not widely available in the early to mid 1940s. Almost every evening people listened to the news on the radio.

Edward R. Murrow reports

Legendary reporter Edward R. Murrow described the scene when he entered Buchenwald, a **concentration camp** where Jews and others died in the **Holocaust.** Rumors had circulated for years that Hitler was torturing and killing in these camps. Now Murrow and other eyewitnesses told the story. It was April 1945.

There surged around me an evil-smelling stink, men and boys reached out to touch me. They were in rags and the remnants of uniforms. Death already had marked many of them, but they were smiling with their eyes . . .

As we walked out into the courtyard, a man fell dead. Two others, they must have been over 60, were crawling toward the latrine [crude toilet]. I saw it, but will not describe it.

In another part of the camp they showed me the children, hundreds of them. Some were only 6 years old. One rolled up his sleeves, showed me his number. It was tattooed on his arm. B-6030, it was. The others showed me their numbers. They will carry them till they die.

We went to the hospital. It was full. The doctor told me that 200 had died the day before . . .

There were two rows of bodies stacked up like cordwood. They were thin and very white. Some of the bodies were terribly bruised . . .

I pray you to believe what I have said about Buchenwald. I reported what I saw and heard, but only part of it. For most of it, I have no words.

If I have offended you by this rather mild account of Buchenwald, I'm not in the least sorry . . .

Sports and Entertainment

During the war, sports and entertainment played significant roles for Americans. Many people were under stress, so being able to laugh, watch talented athletes, escape into a fantasy world, or relax by listening to a favorite song were especially important. Celebrities supported the war effort in a variety of ways. They became leading spokespersons for **war bonds,** entertained troops, contributed money, and even served overseas.

African-American boxer Joe Louis was one of the most popular figures of the time. His graciousness and power as an athlete caused both whites and African Americans to admire him. Louis served in the military during World War II and entertained troops with boxing exhibitions at a variety of sites.

Major League Baseball sluggers Joe DiMaggio and Ted Williams were national heroes during the war years. Like Louis, they served time in the military putting on exhibitions for soldiers. Williams later served in the armed forces again during the Korean War (1950–1953).

Probably no American **civilian** gave more of his time to the military than comedian Bob Hope. The shows he performed for the United Service Organizations (USO) cheered hundreds of thousands of U.S. soldiers stationed overseas during World War II.

At home American **morale** was improved with radio shows, movies, and plays. Almost every family had a radio, and they tuned in to comedy shows such as Abbott and Costello and Red Skelton. A variety of other radio shows, including the news, were also broadcast. Singer Frank Sinatra, the Broadway musicals of Rogers and Hammerstein, and movies were also popular. Some productions, such as movies, were even free for soldiers in uniform.

Joe Louis did much to both support the war effort and gain respect for African Americans.

Soldier letters

Numerous American soldiers wrote letters to Bob Hope during World War II. Below are a few examples.

Well, Mr. Hope,

All the boys over here are in the best of health and they all said to tell you "to keep up the good work on your end of the war" and well will do the same on our end. The folks back home need not to worry—there isn't a one of us who would not go through this invasion for them and we certainly won't let them down.

—Howard L.

Dear Bob,

In a crowded ship, going through sub-infested water it was a big thrill to me to hear the boys laughing their heads off at your jokes. It really brought to us, home, right there in the middle of a damn big ocean. What I'm trying to say, Bob, is that, to us, far, far away from home, you really typify [represent] our way of living and bring us thousands of miles back to our beloved country.

—John M.

The United Service Organizations (USO) was founded in 1941 to provide entertainment and recreation for U.S. military personnel and their families. Here, Bob Hope entertains troops.

The Atomic Bomb

In 1939, President Roosevelt was notified that the Germans were developing an **atomic bomb.** Experts said a single bomb might be able to kill thousands of people. In the early 1940s, facilities at Hanford, Washington, and Oak Ridge, Tennessee, became secret places for the United States to build atomic bombs.

By July 16, 1945, under the supervision of scientist Robert Oppenheimer, an atomic bomb had been produced and tested in the desert near Los Alamos, New Mexico. The result was so terribly powerful that many scientists urged the new president, Harry Truman, not to use it.

President Truman believed several thousand American troops would die if the United States were to invade Japan. He felt that it would be better to use the atomic bomb and end the war quickly, although it would cost thousands of Japanese citizens their lives. Later, Truman stated that more Japanese would probably have been killed if U.S. soldiers invaded, than if the atomic bombs had not been dropped. In the end he chose to use the bomb on Japanese industrial cities. On August 6, 1945, a plane named *Enola Gay* dropped a single atomic bomb on the city of Hiroshima, Japan. Instantly 75,000 people were killed. When the Japanese hesitated to surrender, a second bomb was dropped, killing thousands more in the city of Nagasaki. Five days later, on August 14, the Japanese surrendered.

Atomic bombs created in U.S. factories such as this killed thousands of Japanese civilians. Many victims died slow, painful deaths.

President Harry S. Truman's reasons

Here, Harry S. Truman talks about his decision to use the atomic bomb.

We have used [the bomb] against those who attacked us without warning at Pearl Harbor, against those who have starved and beaten and executed American prisoners, against those who have abandoned all pretense of obeying international laws of warfare. We have used it to shorten the agony of war.

Admiral William D. Leahy's opinion

Admiral William D. Leahy was the senior member of the World War II Joint Chiefs of Staff. Leahy felt that it would have been possible to bring about a Japanese surrender without using the atomic bomb.

It is my opinion that the use of this barbarous [cruel and uncivilized] weapon at Hiroshima and Nagasaki was of no material assistance in our war against Japan. The Japanese were already defeated and ready to surrender ... My own feeling was that in being the first to use it, we had adopted an ethical standard common to the barbarians of the Dark Ages. I was taught not to make war in that fashion, and wars cannot be won by destroying women and children.

Victory

In April 1945 the war ended in Europe. The **Allied Powers** had won. Victory in Europe, or V-E Day, was proclaimed. Four months later, in August 1945, victory over Japan (V-J Day) was declared. What was next? At first, wild celebrations broke out. But people soon realized they would have to adjust to the postwar world.

> " I know the pride that I felt during the war. I just felt ten feet tall. Here I was doing an important job, and doing it well, and then all at once here comes V-J Day, the end of the war, and I'm back making homemade bread [as a housewife]. "
> Frankie Cooper, discussing work after the war.

Italian Americans in New York City wave flags and toss paper into the air as they celebrate the news of Japan's unconditional surrender to the Allies on August 15, 1945.

Sybil Lewis's life after the war

Sybil Lewis was a young girl working in California when the war ended.

The war was over and I knew things were going to change. I realized that the good jobs, all of the advantages that had been offered because of the war, I knew that they were over . . . I said to myself, You came to California to earn enough money to go back to Oklahoma, and now you're going back and complete your education.

James Covert's family

James Covert was a young boy during the war. Both his father and older brother fought in it. Here, he comments on their return.

They [U.S. soldiers] were the winners, the victors; they had fought the war bravely, yet they were disillusioned [unsatisfied]. Those who had some kind of combat experience felt that they had been out there on the front lines, had made great sacrifices, the coming back they found there were not enough houses, and the jobs weren't as plentiful as they thought. So a period of disenchantment [disappointment] set in.

Elliot Johnson's thoughts

Elliot Johnson was in the army when the war ended. After a victory parade in the United States, he had the following thoughts.

I have several close friends who were in the military, and all of us still feel today that we would not take any amount of money for the experience we had. But we still feel that the guys who managed to stay at home came out ahead. I felt then, and still do, a sharp resentment for those men who were able to go but by one means or another avoided going. When I came back, after being gone for four years, they were not only married, but they had purchased their homes, very nice homes. They had made a lot of money, they had started their families, and I was just starting at the beginning and I resented that greatly.

What Have We Learned?

As wars become more modern, the home front increases in importance. United States **civilians** had a tremendous effect on World War II. Technology, a skilled workforce, and intelligent decision making will have even more impact on wars of the future.

Women discovered that their labor could be just as valuable in traditionally male jobs. In some occupations, they found they were better than males. Several female leaders who later fought for equal rights were inspired by advances women made during the war. When women got the chance to help win World War II, they performed brilliantly.

The war meant sacrifice. People saved, conserved, and made efficient use of the materials available. Both the actions and spirit of the U.S. people at home greatly assisted the ultimate victory.

Many U.S. leaders helped by making good decisions and inspiring Americans to stay focused on the job at hand. Franklin Roosevelt will go down in history as a great president, for the confidence he gave people through his fighting spirit. He and others helped people most when the outlook was darkest—the very definition of a great leader.

The home front during World War II proved that wars are won not only by brave heroes, but also through production efforts. Japan and Germany could not hold back the onslaught of the well-equipped **Allied Powers** no matter how hard they fought. And the American workers on the U.S. home front were directly responsible for that production. The often-unrecognized heroics of the common people truly demonstrated that as a nation of states, we were united.

> When the war was over we felt really good about ourselves. We had saved the world from an evil that was unspeakable. . . . I think all of us felt that way. . . . Good times were going to go on and on; everything was going to get better.
> Laura Briggs, on her feelings after World War II ended.

Nancy Harjan remembers 1945

Nancy Harjan was seventeen in 1945. She has vivid memories of the end of World War II in her hometown of San Francisco, California.

I do remember V-E Day. Oh, such a joyous thing! It was in early May. It was my younger brother's birthday and my older brother would most likely be coming home. And San Francisco was chosen for the first session of the UN. . . . Stalin, Churchill, and Roosevelt met, and somehow war never again would happen.

My dad, my younger brother and I, and my mother went to the Sierras for a two-week vacation. In the middle of it came August 6, the bombing of Hiroshima. The war was over. . . .

Within a week or two, bit by bit, it sank in. Seventy thousand or a hundred thousand or two hundred thousand civilians [Japanese killed]? It came as a shock after seeing so many war movies with the Japanese portrayed as militaristic brutes. To see women, children, and old innocent civilians brutally burned . . .

As the war came to an end, I was totally blown away by how quickly our former enemies became our friends and how quickly our former friends became our enemies. I couldn't understand that. I began to ask, What was it all about?

During World War II, people of all races pulled together to work on the U.S. war effort. The work of ordinary civilians aided greatly in the Allies victory.

Timeline

1939 September 1: Germany invades Poland starting World War II
September 3: Britain and France declare war on Germany

1940 September: U.S. Congress passes the draft requiring all men between ages 21 and 35 to register and be eligible to fight
November: Franklin D. Roosevelt is elected president for the third time

1941 March 11: Congress passes the **Lend-Lease Act,** allowing the U.S. to sell supplies to **allies** with "delayed payment"
May: Lack of job opportunities cause A. Philip Randolph to call for a huge protest. The protest was cancelled when Roosevelt issued an order to stop unfair treatment of **minorities** in the workplace.
December 7: Japan attacks Pearl Harbor
December 8: The United States, Great Britain, and Canada declare war on Japan

1942 February: Roosevelt orders 110,000 Japanese-Americans be relocated to **internment camps**
June 4–6: The U.S. defeats Japan in the Battle of Midway—a turning point in the war

1944 January: More personal injuries occur in U.S. factories than on the battlefields
June 6: D-Day invasion occurs on the north coast of France (Normandy)
July: Willow Run aircraft factory near Detroit turns out a B-24 bomber every 63 minutes and 10,000-ton (9,072-metric ton) Liberty ships are being launched on the West Coast at the rate of two a day
December: Thirty-six percent of the U.S. workforce is female

1945 February 19: U.S. marines fight their way into Iwo Jima, very close to the mainland of Japan
April 12: Franklin Roosevelt dies. Vice President Harry S. Truman becomes president
May 7: Germany surrenders and World War II in Europe ends
August 6: The U.S. drops an **atomic bomb** on Hiroshima, Japan
August 9: The U.S. drops a second atomic bomb on Nagasaki, Japan
August 14: Japan agrees to end the war
September 2: Representatives of Japan sign the official statement of surrender. President Truman declares V-J Day (Victory over Japan day) and World War II ends.

List of Primary Sources

The author and publisher gratefully acknowledge the following publications and websites from which written sources in this book are drawn. In some cases, the wording or sentence structure has been simplified to make the material more appropriate for a school readership.

p. 9 Franklin D. Roosevelt: State of the Union address, January 6, 1942.

p. 11 Franklin D. Roosevelt: *No Ordinary Time—Franklin and Eleanor Roosevelt: The Home Front in World War II*, Doris Kearns Goodwin (New York: Simon & Schuster, 1994).

p. 13 Thomas Scott: *The Home Front: America During World War II*, Mark J. Harris, Franklin D. Mitchell, and Steven J. Schechter (New York: Putnam's and Sons, 1984).
Sheril Jankovsky Cunning: *The Home Front: America During World War II*, Mark J. Harris, Franklin D. Mitchell, and Steven J. Schechter (New York: Putnam's and Sons, 1984).

p. 15 W. Lloyd Warner: *Democracy in Jonesville*, W. Lloyd Warner (New York: Harper, 1949).

p. 17 Shirley Hackett: *The Home Front: America During World War II*, Mark J. Harris, Franklin D. Mitchell, and Steven J. Schechter (New York: Putnam's and Sons, 1984).

p. 21 Eleanor Roosevelt: www.quotationspage.com.

p. 23 Don Johnson: *No Ordinary Time—Franklin and Eleanor Roosevelt: The Home Front in World War II*, Doris Kearns Goodwin (New York: Simon & Schuster, 1994).

p. 25 Frankie Cooper: *The Home Front: America During World War II*, Mark J. Harris, Franklin D. Mitchell, and Steven J. Schechter (New York: Putnam's and Sons, 1984).

p. 27 Laura Briggs: *No Ordinary Time—Franklin and Eleanor Roosevelt: The Home Front in World War II*, Doris Kearns Goodwin (New York: Simon & Schuster, 1994).

p. 29 Sybil Lewis: *The Home Front: America During World War II*, Mark J. Harris, Franklin D. Mitchell, and Steven J. Schechter (New York: Putnam's and Sons, 1984).

p. 31 Vernon Sietmann: *The Home Front: America During World War II*, Mark J. Harris, Franklin D. Mitchell, and Steven J. Schechter (New York: Putnam's and Sons, 1984).

p. 33 Frankie Cooper: *The Home Front: America During World War II*, Mark J. Harris, Franklin D. Mitchell, and Steven J. Schechter (New York: Putnam's and Sons, 1984).

p. 33 Sybil Lewis: *The Home Front: America During World War II*, Mark J. Harris, Franklin D. Mitchell, and Steven J. Schechter (New York: Putnam's and Sons, 1984).

p. 35 Accounts from the family of Albert and Louise Wood: *The Home Front: U.S.A.*, Ronald H. Bailey and the editors of Time-Life Books (Alexandria, Va.: Time-Life Books, 1978).

p. 37 Jean Barr: personal account written in April 2003 at request of author.

p. 39 Alexander Allen: *The Home Front: America During World War II*, Mark J. Harris, Franklin D. Mitchell, and Steven J. Schechter (New York: Putnam's and Sons, 1984).

p. 41 Margaret Takahashi: *The Home Front: America During World War II*, Mark J. Harris, Franklin D. Mitchell, and Steven J. Schechter (New York: Putnam's and Sons, 1984).
Arthur Morimitsu: *A History of the United States: American Voices*, Carol Berkin, Alan Brinkley, Clayborne Carson, Robert W. Cherny, Robert A. Divine, Eric Foner, Jefferey B. Morris, Reverend Arthur Wheeler, and Leonard Wood (Glenview, Ill.: Scott Foresman, 1992).

p. 43 Edward R. Murrow: *PM*, April 16, 1945. "They Died 900 a Day in 'the Best' Nazi Death Camp."

p. 45 Howard L.: www.bobhope.com/bhletters.html.
John M.: www.bobhope.com/bhletters.html.

p. 47 Harry Truman: *A History of the United States: American Voices*, Carol Berkin, Alan Brinkley, Clayborne Carson, Robert W. Cherny, Robert A. Divine, Eric Foner, Jefferey B. Morris, Reverend Arthur Wheeler, and Leonard Wood (Glenview, Ill.: Scott Foresman, 1992).
Admiral William D. Leahy: www.spectacle.org.

p. 49 Sybil Lewis: *The Home Front: America During World War II*, Mark J. Harris, Franklin D. Mitchell, and Steven J. Schechter (New York: Putnam's and Sons, 1984).
James Covert: *The Home Front: America During World War II*, Mark J. Harris, Franklin D. Mitchell, and Steven J. Schechter (New York: Putnam's and Sons, 1984).
Eliot Johnson: *The Home Front: America During World War II*, Mark J. Harris, Franklin D. Mitchell, and Steven J. Schechter (New York: Putnam's and Sons, 1984).

p. 51 Nancy Harjan: *The Good War: An Oral History of World War Two*, Studs Terkel (New York: Pantheon Books, 1984).

Glossary

Allied Powers during World War II, Great Britain, France, the United States, and the Soviet Union

ally person or nation associated or united with another in a common purpose

ambassador person sent as the chief representative of his or her government in another country

anti-aircraft gun quick-firing, small cannon designed to shoot down airplanes

atomic bomb bomb whose great power is due to the sudden release of the energy in the nuclei of atoms

Axis Powers military forces of Germany, Italy, Japan, and the countries that fought with them during World War II

bias existing opinion about someone or something that makes it hard to be fair

bigotry belief in only one opinion; unable to accept another's beliefs or practices

blackout curtain window hanging that prevents light from escaping

campaign series of military operations in a certain area or for a certain purpose; series of activities meant to get a certain thing done, such as an election

civilian person not on active duty in a military, police, or fire-fighting force

civil defense group of government officials that was responsible for guarding borders and preparing U.S. citizens for possible enemy attacks

commander in chief person who holds supreme command of the armed forces of a nation

compensation something, such as money, that makes up for or is given to make up for something else

concentration camp prison camp set up by the Nazis under a special law that meant that prisoners were never tried and were never given a release date

death camp camp set up by the Nazis to murder as many people, most of them Jewish, as quickly and as cheaply as possible

dictator person who has absolute control of a government

discrimination treating people better or unfairly because of their differences, such as race or gender

dust bowl region that suffers from prolonged droughts and dust storms

Fascism form of government usually headed by a dictator in which the government controls most aspects of the people's lives

finance provide money for

government agency group that works in certain area of the U.S. government to make sure things run smoothly

Great Depression worldwide economic downturn of the 1930s

Holocaust attempt by Nazi government in Germany to destroy all of the Jewish people in their power

income tax tax on the income of a person or business

interest amount charged for the right to use or borrow money

internment camp temporary holding area for groups thought to be a threat

isolationism policy of staying completely out of the affairs of other nations

Lend-Lease Act created by President Roosevelt during World War II that allowed the U.S. to send supplies to Great Britain and other allies and let them pay later

minority part of a population that is in some ways different from others and that is sometimes disliked or given unfair treatment

monopoly complete control of the entire supply of goods or a service in a certain market; complete possession

morale condition of the mind or feelings—in relation to enthusiasm, spirit, or hope—of an individual or group

Nazi member of the National Socialist German Workers' Party; supporter of Adolf Hitler

newsreel short motion picture about current events

policy course of action chosen to guide people in making decisions

polio once common viral disease often affecting children and sometimes causing paralysis

prejudice belief that one group is superior to another

propaganda organized spreading of certain ideas; or the ideas spread in such a way

racist person who believes that a certain race is better than another

rationing distributing certain amounts of food or other supplies

raw material basic material needed to produce goods

Revolutionary War American fight for independence from British rule between 1775–1783

Roman Empire lands and people under the rule of ancient Rome

sabotage secretly using violent and destructive acts; one who performs sabotage is a *saboteur*

segregation forced separation of a race, class, or ethnic group

slogan word or phrase used by a party, group, or business to attract attention

State of the Union address annual speech given by the President of the United States to the American people discussing current status of the nation

stereotype fixed idea that many people have about a thing or group and may often by untrue or only partially true

strike temporary stoppage of work in protest against an act or condition

symbolic relating to something that stands for something else

Union Nations association of countries formed in 1945 to promote world peace

victory garden garden created by U.S. civilians during World War II in which the crops were given to the U.S. Armed Forces (to feed troops)

war bond piece of paper bought from the government during wartime to raise money. A bond could be sold back to the government several years later in order to receive more money than was originally paid.

Sources for Further Research

Barr, Gary. *Pearl Harbor*. Chicago: Heinemann Library, 2004.

Connolly, Sean. *World War II*. Chicago: Heinemann Library, 2003.

Dowswell, Paul. *The Causes of World War II*. Chicago: Heinemann Library, 2003.

Tames, Richard. *Hiroshima: The Shadow of the Bomb*. Chicago: Heinemann Library, 2000.

Tames, Richard. *Pearl Harbor: The U.S. Enters World War II*. Chicago: Heinemann Library, 2000.

Taylor, David. *Franklin D. Roosevelt*. Chicago: Heinemann Library, 2001.

Index